THE RIVERBANK GANG

Written by Richard Wilmot

Illustrated by Howard Molloy

FOR JAMIE

Printed in the UK by TAS Offset Ltd, Norwich. Designed, produced and published by Wilmot Bill Ltd.

STORY 1.

The Rebellion

The Rebellion

It was near dead of night when the meeting commenced,
On a still, moonlit river bank,
The animals waited, upright and tense,
All seated in order of rank.

Their Chairman, a fat-bellied frog of repute,
Who sat perched on a large, rotting oak
Wore a red buttoned waistcoat, a black velvet topper
And a beautiful green-spotted cloak.

As he chatted, his many chins wobbled around
And his top hat slid over one ear,
But no one dared giggle, or utter a sound
For his temper was something to fear.

Next to Frog sat King Rat, a more elderly gent,
Who was even more snappily dressed,
In a white tie and tails with a long centre vent
Beneath which you could just see his vest.

In his mouth was a large, brown Havana cigar
And his hands clasped an old walking stick,
But everyone knew that the Rat was no fool,
For his age he was agile and quick.

The Frog then leaned over and whispered to Rat,
"Perhaps it's time that we outlined our plan,"
To which Rat gently nodded, and so reassured,
Chairman Frog cleared his throat and began.

"Gentlemen," he croaked in theatrical tone,
"We have called you all here after dark
To discuss the town's plans to plunder our homes
And erect a new Pleasure Boat Park."

"Such a park" he continued, "as I'm sure you're aware,
Would endanger our very existence,
So King Rat has proposed that we all band together,
And devise our most spirited resistance."

MATTY

They all listened; the Eel and Dan Dragonfly,
Matty Mole, the Moorhen and Snake
Then they chatted together and tried to agree
On exactly what action to take.
Till the Snake, slithering over to Frog and King Rat
Said; "Asss Ssspokesman, it'sss my duty to sssay,
We're unanimousss! No pleasure boatsss and that'sss that!
We're behind you every inch of the way."
Chairman Frog proudly smiled at his colleague King Rat,
Who lit up a celebratory cigar,
And the meeting concluded just as the sun rose
And church bells began chiming from afar.
It was later that day that three council officials
Were expected to visit the river,
To conclude a report on the Pleasure Park issue,
A report they would never deliver.

King Rat, although old, was a man of great strength
And there was no better swimmer alive,
His underwater record for swimming the length
Of the stream, had for ten years survived.

So the task Frog had given him was easily done,
"See that small power boat, my good fella,
Take one end of this water reed Moorhen is holding,
And tie it around and around the propellor!"
Moorhen then circled an old weeping willow
And tying a huge sailor's knot,
Settled back, with a used baked-bean tin for a pillow,
To await the unfolding of the plot.

Meanwhile, Matty Mole and Dan Dragonfly,
Had hit on a wheeze more severe,
They had turned round a sign that read:
'MOORINGS THIS WAY,'
And re-directed it straight towards the weir.

But for cunning and guile there was nothing to match,
The unscrupulous plan hatched by Eel,
Who had looped a large magnet around the branch of a tree,
With the help of an old fishing reel.

At four thirty, three obese-looking councillors arrived
And clumsily boarded the boat,

As the huge VIP's plonked themselves side by side,
The poor craft only just stayed afloat.

The engine first spluttered, then splattered, then coughed,
Then finally roared off upstream,
And innocently our three bloated men in a boat,
Journeyed off where no others had been.

But only a few yards had the three of them travelled,
When the boat lunged, then jerked to a halt.
And the propellor propelled itself into the air,
Like a stone from a large catapult.

The three scarlet officials, their clothes all askew,
Panic-stricken, made a grab for the oars,
"It's fast running water but with these we'll get through,"
Said one, scrambling around on all fours.

As they paddled and panicked, all the animals laughed,
(Which was quite understandable on reflection)
For it was just as if three bulls had been put in the craft
And told to pull in three different directions.
Then one councilman suddenly jumped up and shouted,
"Oh look, there's a sign that says 'MOORINGS,'
If we make one big effort to turn her about,
We may find a place to secure in."
But then just as suddenly, the going got easier
And the boat seemed to glide on it's own,
Then it quickened and sped and went faster and faster,
With three passengers who wished they'd stayed home.
As they hurtled along gripping tight to the boat,
One said, "What's that ahead? It's a weir!"
"Oh no!" choked the first; "Oh dear!" yelled the second
And the third said, "I do feel quite queer!"

The boat was now racing, caught up in the current
And spinning around more and more
And a terrible fate was becoming apparent,
Unless they could make it ashore.

So they frantically heaved and tugged at the oars,
In one last desperate bid for survival,
Till they came level with Eel, a huge grin on his face,
As he eagerly awaited their arrival.

From the tree, the giant magnet hung menacingly
And as three scared officials passed below,
Eel's truly magnetic personality,
Yanked them out of the water like minnows.

The metal rings on the oars clung to the magnet
Like leeches, and below the men hung,
All swinging precariously backwards and forwards,
Like a grandfather clock's pendulum.

And there they remained, till was gathered beneath them
The whole riverside population,
There was Frog and King Rat, Mole, Snake and the others,
All dancing in wild celebration.

It is said the officials, bedraggled and dazed,
Were eventually rescued that night
And were taken for rest and some recuperation,
Before revealing details of their plight.

Now the text of their story was never disclosed,
But its consequence is animal folklore,
One single column article in the Priggish Town Post, read:

COUNCIL'S PLEASURE PARK
PLANS – OUT THE DOOR.

STORY 2.

The One-Day Excursion.

PETROL

The One-Day Excursion

*Chairman Frog was dressed up in his Sunday best waistcoat
And his favourite black velvet topper,
A green spotted coat that he'd had specially pressed
And a scarlet bow tie with a popper.*

*As he stood, his fat paunch falling over his pants,
A bright twinkle seemed to glint in his eyes
And his face was aglow with a broad, childish grin,
He was obviously bursting with pride.*

*For today was the day he'd reveal to his friends,
The secret he'd kept for some time,
Why he'd hammered and banged for three whole weekends
And why he'd ordered <u>three</u> new washing lines.*

*Rumours had been rife around the whole river bank,
That the mystery was about to unravel
And a crowd was expected at Frog's petrol tank home,
Half submerged in the waterside gravel.*

Frog sat on top of the rusty brown tank,
Near the hole where the petrol cap had been,
A hole that was now a grandiose front door,
Decked with lillies and reeds of dark green.

The first to arrive was Dan Dragonfly,
His busy wings whirring aloud,
On his long matchstick body a red shirt and tie,
He said; "I'll sit on this stone if I'm allowed."

Chairman Frog nodded 'yes' and Dan duly sat down,
Swiftly joined by a smart Matty Mole,
Who had swum up unnoticed by the rest of his pals,
From a freshly dug underwater hole.
Just a few moments passed and then Skinny Shrew appeared,
And settled back on a moss-covered log,
"Hello Matty, hello Dan," he said stroking his beard,
"And good-day to you, Chairman Frog."

Then up swam Olly Otter, his long bushy tail
A perfect and speedy propellor
And last, but not least, proud portly King Rat,
Frog said, "Glad you could come, my good fella."
King Rat had splashed out on some sparkling new clothes,
Gone his usual tails and tight breeches,
For a stunning cream suit with a massive red rose
And black shoes with neat yellow stitches.

Chairman Frog smiled a welcome to all of his friends,
Then he briskly jumped up on his feet,
"Fellow waterside dwellers, I'm so glad you made it.
I assure you, you're in for a treat.

You may have been wondering about the terrible row,
All the banging and clanging you've heard,
Well, I think when you see the results of my labour,
You'll be glad no one protested a word."

With that, Chairman Frog proudly beckoned his pals
And led them along his back path
And there, in the sunlight, with a handkerchief sail,
Bobbed a beautiful, new wooden raft.

TONKA

Twelve assorted chair legs roped securely together,
A small wooden kitchen spoon rudder,
An obsolete garden-hoe handle for a mast,
And plush seats from one end to the other.

Chairman Frog's hand-built craft stood resplendant before them,
The whole group quite speechless with joy,
Till the silence was broken by a beaming King Rat,
"I think you've worked wonders, my boy."

"It's a masterful job," chipped in Matty the Mole,
"A triumph," roared Skinny the Shrew,
"Now I think we should open a bottle," said Rat,
"For I have a proposal for you."

Rat swam off at speed but was back in a trice,
In his hands a large bottle of champagne,
Then, producing a can full of small chunks of ice,
He settled down with the others again.

He shakingly poured all his pals ample drinks, still trembling from his over-exertion,

Then said, "Gentleman, what does everyone think
About us going on A ONE-DAY EXCURSION?"

"A trip," he continued, "a mystery tour,
To discover what lies far upstream,
We'll probably see things we've never dreamt of before,
Visit places where no one has been."

Rat's small band of animal friends were all ears
And his question was answered there and then,
For they jumped up as one and gave three rousing cheers,
Rat smiled, "Great, now we must decide when."

The following morning, before crack of dawn,
Six shadowy figures set sail
And as a southerly breeze gently whisked them along,
They all prayed that good weather would prevail.

Mile after mile, the tall mast almost bending,
Past wierd-looking hedgerows they danced,
Along stretches of river that seemed never-ending,
Our intrepid explorers advanced.

And every so often a strange face would peer out,
From a stone or the roots of a tree,
Then, as fast as it came it would vanish forever,
Like a mirage they would never again see.

"When I was a lad," mused Frog to the rest,
"I heard tales of some rapids quite near."
"Well they were just stories," snapped Rat, "I suggest
You don't believe everything that you hear!"

Frog forgot all about it, admiring the view,
A friendly weasel doffed his hat from the land,
A watersnake called out; "Good morning to you,"
As they passed, what a pleasant young man!

The animals relaxed on their round jam jar seats,
And the trip seemed a roaring success,
Matty, leaning back said, "This little adventure beats
Sitting around our place I guess."

But as he peered at the sky, his heart slowly sank,
For now it wasn't the blue it had been,
But a dark, murky brown, just like Frog's petrol tank
And a huge shadow engulfed the whole scene.
"See those clouds," shouted Matty pointing up
with his arm,
"We're in for a storm, sure enough,"
"Well, if we prepare ourselves we'll come to no harm,"
Answered Rat, "But it might get quite rough.

So Matty take this rope, tie it tight around your waist,
Then pass it to Dan who'll do the same,
Then Olly and so on, but do it in haste,
For I've just felt the first drop of rain."
As Rat spoke, a giant rain droplet hit Chairman Frog,
Almost knocking his velvet top hat off,
But the others just carried on securing themselves,
They were all far too worried to scoff.

When the wet rope was finally tied around everyone,
King Rat looped it twice around the mast
And after expertly tying a huge sailor's knot
Said, "Now hang on till the danger has passed."
As he spoke, the heavens opened above the small raft
And a terrible storm was upon them,
Huge rain drops like cannonballs bombarded the craft,
Causing the tiny crew all kinds of problems.
As the current raced frantically this way and that,
Giant waves began pounding the bank,
Then rebounding against the small craft with a "Splaaat!"
And more than once the explorers almost sank.
"Keep your heads!" Rat was screaming above the fierce wind,
Which was swirling the raft round and round,
"It will soon all blow over, have courage my friends,"
He insisted, though his voice was half drowned.

Then, suddenly, before them a bigger threat loomed,
The rapids that riverfolk warned of,
All the animals panicked, for they thought they were doomed,
"I d...d...don't think we'll make it," stuttered Frog.

Matty Mole and Dan Dragonfly collided with each other,
Both looking decidedly green
And poor Olly who wished he was back home with mother,
Couldn't even raise enough breath to scream.

The tiny craft hurtled downstream such a pace,
That all the bumping and lurching around,
Sent poor Chairman Frog flying flat on his face,
Almost crushing Skinny Shrew to the ground.

Then the raft hit a rock with a deafening THUMP!
Then another, sending Matty reeling forward,
He tumbled headlong, hit his nose with a bump,
Bounced and ended up SPLASH! overboard.

Chairman Frog, staying calm, found the raft's only lifebelt,
A rubber tyre from a child's Tonka van,
Tied a rope to it, attaching one end to himself,
Then hurled it, holding tightly to Dan.

The current was dangerously swirling and seething
And Matty disappeared like a float,
Leaving only a few bubbles to prove he was breathing
And a button that had torn loose from his coat.

The lifebelt had landed right over the bubbles
And to everyone's relief, first a tail,
Then a water-sodden head emerged from the swell,
Spouting water in a fountain like a whale.

Matty grabbed the rubber tyre, splashing out with his arms,
Gurgling, "I've got it Frog, p..p..please pull me in."
"Hold on tight," Frog yelled back, "and you'll come to no harm,"
But his assurance was lost in the wind.

They were still in the rapids and what fate would befall them,
Not even wise King Rat could say,
Till Olly, looking skyward, began rushing around calling,
"It's stopping...the clouds are clearing away."

The drenched crew looked up and there sure enough,
A small patch of blue had appeared,
Now the river was definitely not quite so rough
And the rapids had almost been cleared.

"Just pray our luck holds for another half minute,"
Murmured Rat, "and we'll all be OK,
Olly's right, the wind's dropped, look the sail's got none in it,
The danger's almost over, I'd say."

Then as fast as it started, the storm ebbed and died
And a beautiful calm took its place,
The animals' raft began simply to glide
Down the river at a leisurely pace.

Frog picked himself up and stood dripping and flushed,
Then Olly clambered up on his feet,
Joined by Skinny and Dan, then Matty who rushed
Up to Rat to shake hands with relief.

The happy band all threw their arms around each other
And danced about the raft cheering loudly,
"I think we should now look for suitable cover,
And somewhere to moor," said Rat proudly.

Chairman Frog and the rest all nodded their agreement
And they steered for an old wooden bridge,
There they tethered the raft around a block of cement,
And climbed on to a small grassy ridge.

Within minutes, their clothes had been hung up to dry
And they huddled in a circle together,
Chairman Frog muttered, "Well, we gave it a try
And perhaps it would have worked with better weather.

But I suggest we now find an alternative route
And set off for home my good friends,
This excursion was one trip I'll never forget,
BUT DON'T ANYONE DARE SUGGEST IT AGAIN!"

THE END